The LEGO® Batman Movie
Official Annual 2018

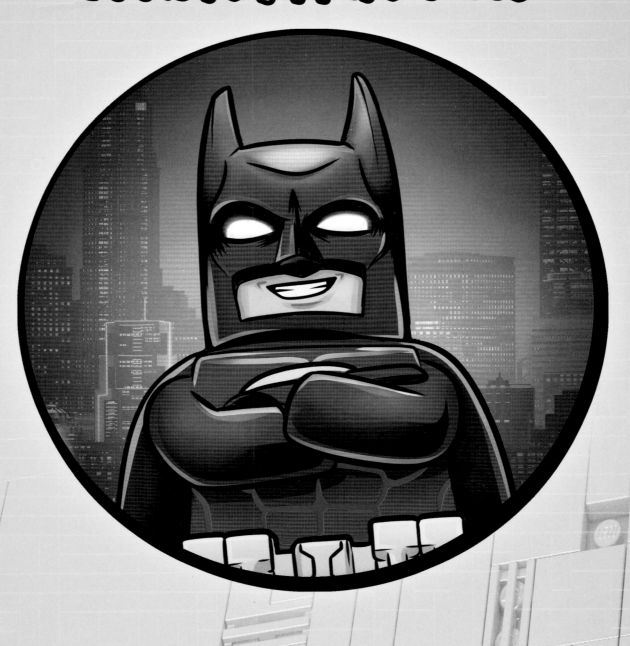

EGMONT

CONTENTS

7

ROBIN'S FIRST PATROL

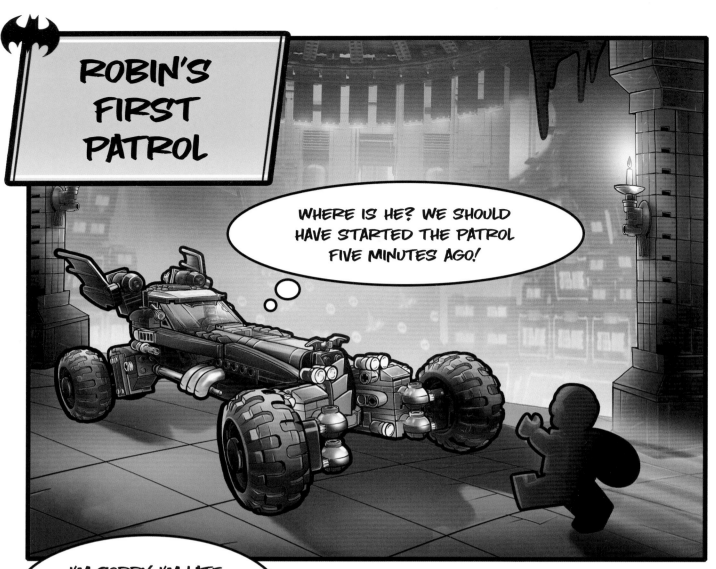

WHERE IS HE? WE SHOULD HAVE STARTED THE PATROL FIVE MINUTES AGO!

I'M SORRY I'M LATE. WE CAN GO NOW. WOW, I'M SUPER EXCITED, THIS IS MY ...

HAVEN'T YOU FORGOTTEN SOMETHING?

I SAID I WAS SORRY ...

FINISH

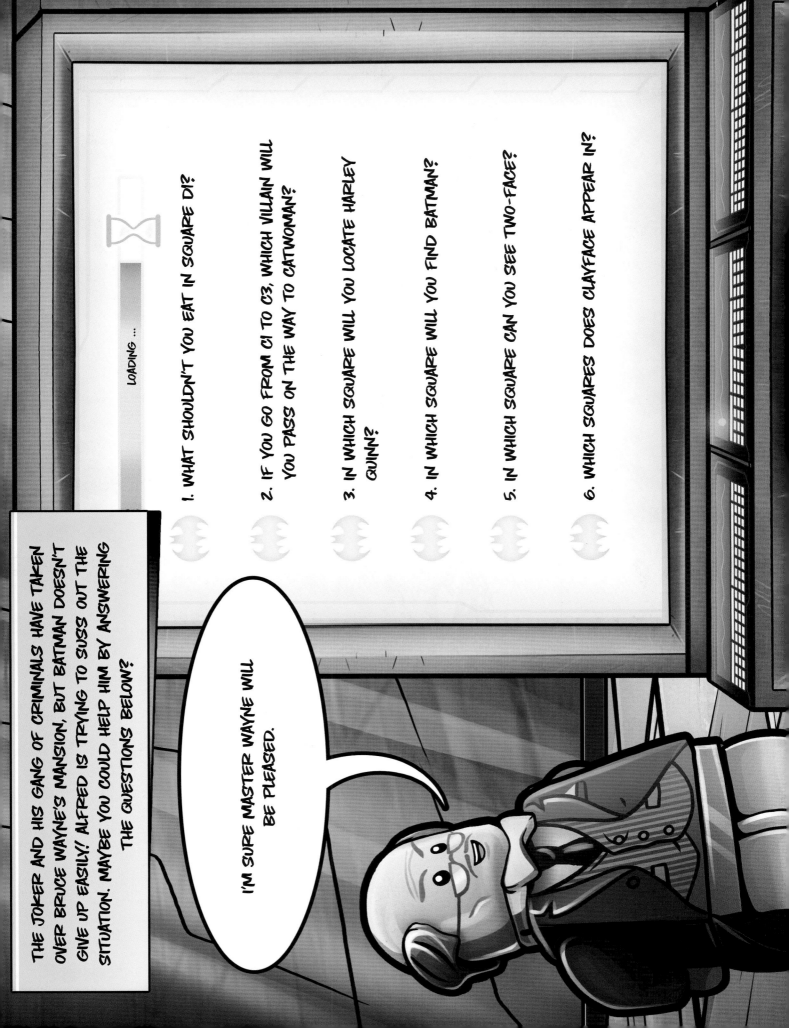

WHOSE COMBAT VEHICLE?

WHOSE VEHICLE IS GUARDING THE ENTRANCE TO WAYNE MANOR? CIRCLE THE ANSWER OPPOSITE. THEN FIND THE OWNER OF THE VEHICLE AND TWO OTHER VILLAINS ON THE PAGE.

FALCONE'S
LEGIT CONSTRUCTION C

MR. FREEZE'S PUZZLE

MR. FREEZE IS GETTING READY TO PURSUE BATMAN! LOOK CAREFULLY AT THE ICY SHAPES THE MASTER OF COLD HAS MADE, AND COUNT THE NUMBER OF TRIANGLES EACH OF THEM CONTAINS. WHEN YOU'VE FINISHED, FIND BATMAN AND BATGIRL IN THE PICTURE.

A =

B =

C =

D =

A

B

REAL DIAMONDS

WHEN THE CROOKS BROKE INTO THE TREASURY, THE REAL DIAMONDS GOT MUDDLED UP WITH THE FAKE ONES! FIRST, FIND THE SEVEN REAL ONES. THEN, COUNT THE CROWNS AND TREASURE CHESTS.

GET THE JOKER
FOLLOW THE ARROWS TO HELP BATMAN CATCH THE JOKER! NOTE, THE ARROWS ALL HAVE TO POINT IN THE DIRECTION YOU NEED TO GO IN. NEXT, FIND OUT WHICH OF THE PICTURE PIECES DOESN'T MATCH THE JOKER'S CAR.
FINISH
BUT THAT'S MY JOB! HA HA HA!
Joker

THE PENGUIN'S ESCAPE

THE PENGUIN IS TRYING TO ESCAPE!
BUT BATMAN WON'T LET HIM GET AWAY.

CONNECT THE DOTS TO SEE
WHAT THE PENGUIN FORGOT
TO TAKE WITH HIM.

30

DOCTOR'S SECRET

UNTANGLE THE LINES TO FIND OUT WHICH VILLAIN IS A PSYCHIATRIST WHEN SHE TAKES OFF HER MASK.

CATWOMAN

POISON IVY

HARLEY QUINN

HA HA HA HA

BATTLE PICS

WILL ROBIN AND BATGIRL BE ABLE TO HANDLE
THE MIGHTY KILLER CROC? BATMAN HAS TAUGHT
THEM ALL SORTS OF TRICKS. CIRCLE THE SMALL
PICTURES WHEN YOU FIND THEM IN THE SCENE.

NOW FIND FOUR SUPER-VILLAINS HIDING
IN THE CROWD.

33

LOST WEAPONS

A STREET FIGHT IS IN PROGRESS. HELP BATMAN FIND ALL THE WEAPONS THE SUPER-VILLAINS ARE THINKING ABOUT. CAN YOU FIND MAN-BAT?

WHY I SHOULD BE BATMAN'S NEMESIS!

BY THE JOKER

I'M SURE YOU ALL KNOW ME BY NOW. I AM THE JOKER AND I'M ABOUT TO EXPLAIN WHY I AM BATMAN'S GREATEST ENEMY ...

1. I AM A NATURAL CRIMINAL LEADER!

2. MY CAR IS A REAL FOUR-WHEELED MONSTER! (WELL, OCCASIONALLY THREE-WHEELED.)

3. ONCE I STOOD UP TO SUPERMAN! (ADMITTEDLY, IT PROBABLY WASN'T THE BEST IDEA I'VE EVER HAD.)

4. MY GADGETS ARE EQUALLY AS IMPRESSIVE AS BATMAN'S.

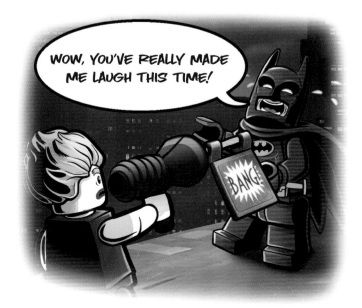

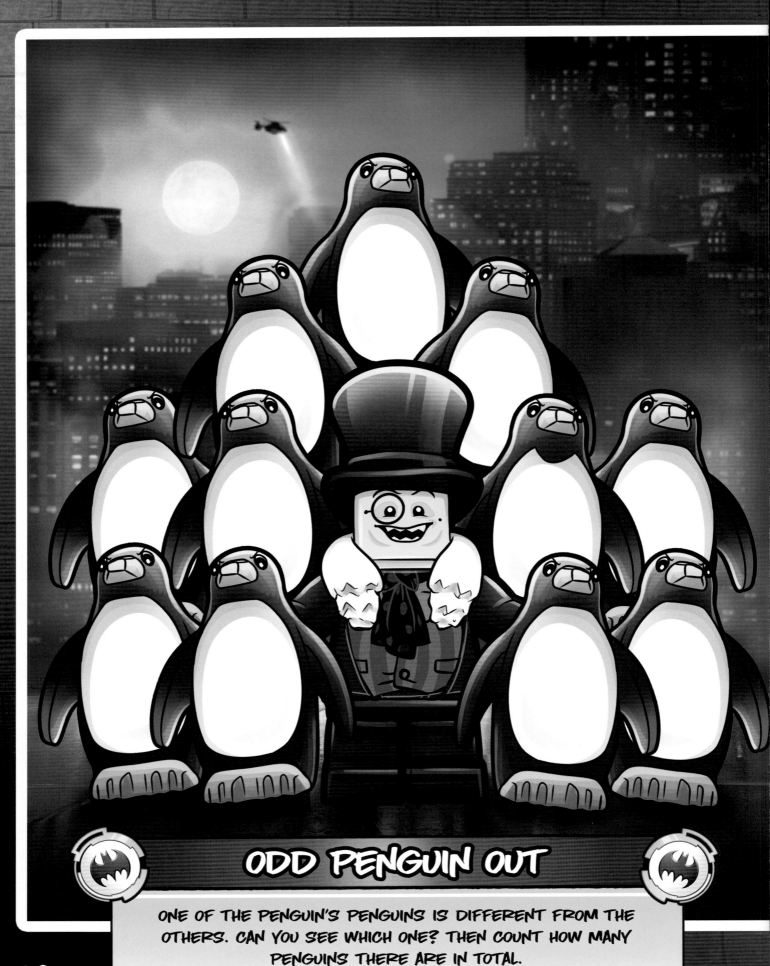

ODD PENGUIN OUT

ONE OF THE PENGUIN'S PENGUINS IS DIFFERENT FROM THE OTHERS. CAN YOU SEE WHICH ONE? THEN COUNT HOW MANY PENGUINS THERE ARE IN TOTAL.

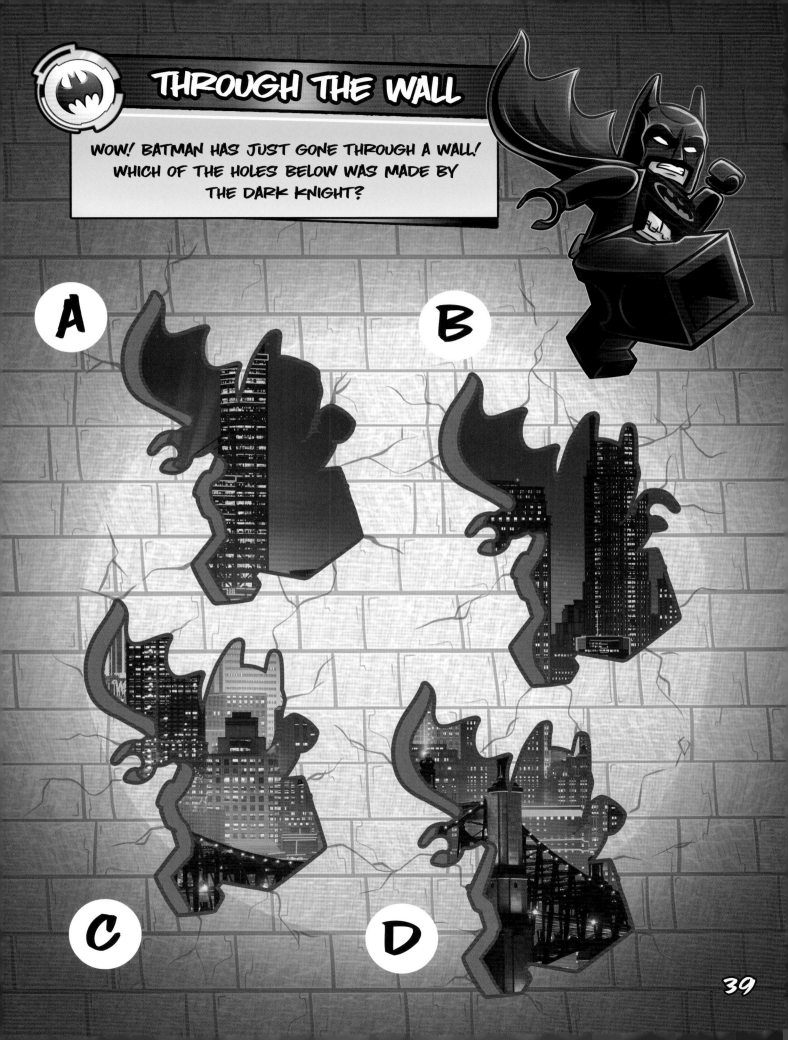

THROUGH THE WALL

WOW! BATMAN HAS JUST GONE THROUGH A WALL! WHICH OF THE HOLES BELOW WAS MADE BY THE DARK KNIGHT?

A

B

C

D

MISSING BATARANGS

HOW MANY BATARANGS CAN YOU FIND IN THIS MESS? =

STOP THE PENGUIN!

ONLY ONE OF THESE PARTS CAME FROM THE PENGUIN'S VEHICLE. CAN YOU FIND IT BEFORE BATMAN REACHES THE SCOUNDREL?

A

B

C

NOW FIND FOUR PENGUINS HIDING AROUND HERE.

43

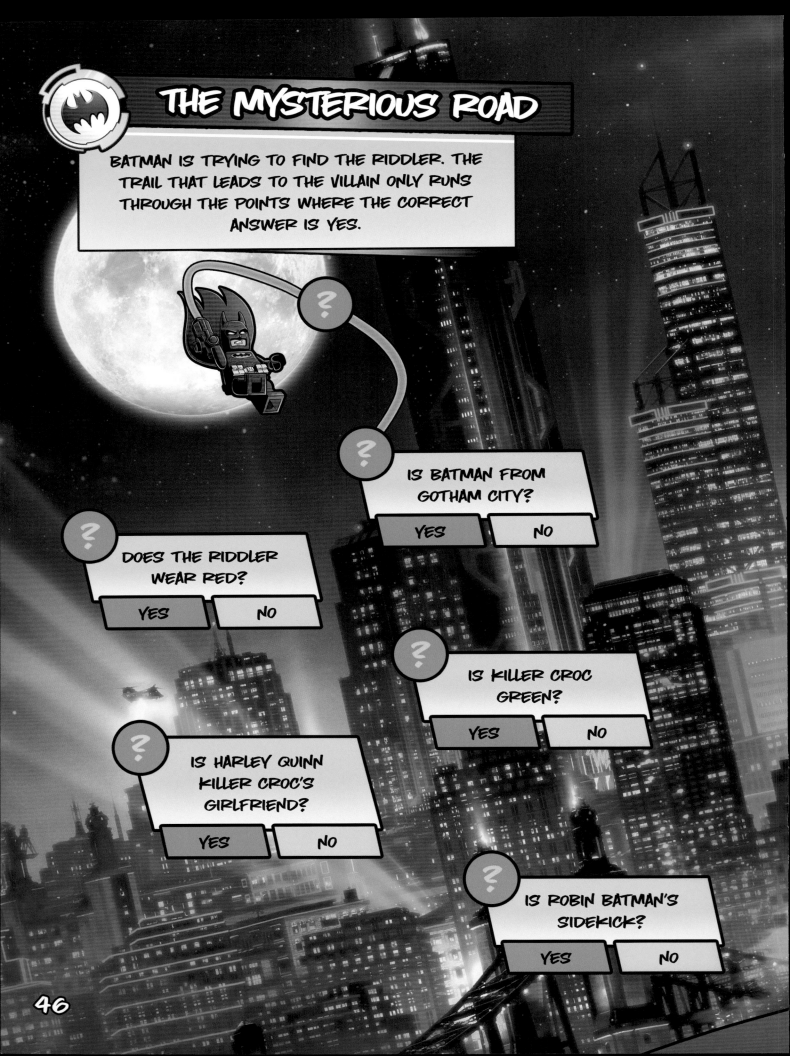

THE MYSTERIOUS ROAD

BATMAN IS TRYING TO FIND THE RIDDLER. THE TRAIL THAT LEADS TO THE VILLAIN ONLY RUNS THROUGH THE POINTS WHERE THE CORRECT ANSWER IS YES.

IS BATMAN FROM GOTHAM CITY?
YES   NO

DOES THE RIDDLER WEAR RED?
YES   NO

IS KILLER CROC GREEN?
YES   NO

IS HARLEY QUINN KILLER CROC'S GIRLFRIEND?
YES   NO

IS ROBIN BATMAN'S SIDEKICK?
YES   NO

47

FIND THE JOKER

THE JOKER HAS DRESSED UP LOTS OF CLOWNS TO LOOK EXACTLY LIKE HIM. ALL THAT EFFORT TO DECEIVE BATMAN! BUT ONLY ONE OF THEM IS THE REAL JOKER. WHICH ONE IS IT?

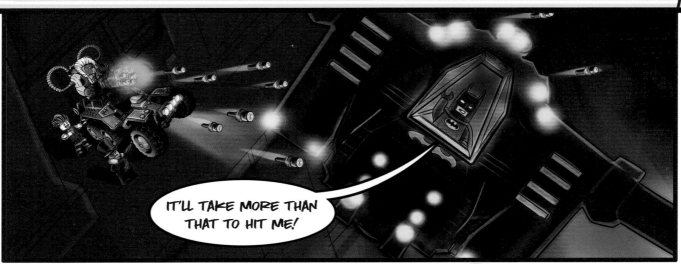

BAT-PUZZLE

TIME TO TACKLE A TASK! CAN YOU LABEL THE PIECES FROM A-G TO MAKE THE FINISHED PICTURE? WE'VE ADDED 'A' ALREADY TO GET YOU STARTED ...

A

"The Speedwagon"

I ONLY NEED FIVE SECONDS TO DO IT, BUT I AM BATMAN AFTER ALL!

ANSWERS

8-9
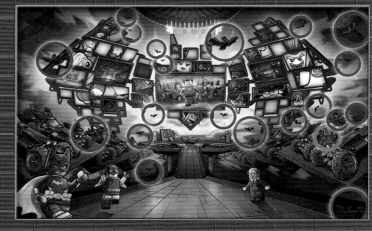

6-7
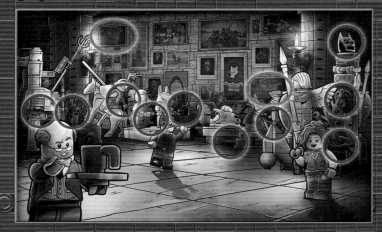

12-13

14-15

20-21

18-19: 1. TOXIC PIZZA
     2. BANE
     3. D5

4. B6
5. A3
6. B5, C5, C6, D5, D6

22-23: A = 11, B = 12, C = 13, D = 11

24-25: 5 CROWNS, 8 CHESTS

26-27

28-29: 10 BATARANGS

31

30

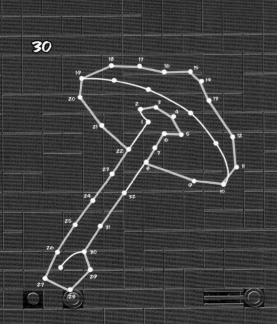

32-33

34-35

39: C

38: 11 PENGUINS

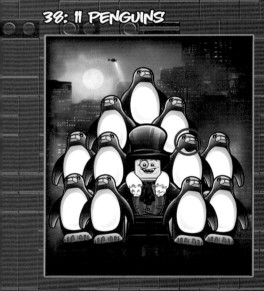

40-41: 8 BATARANGS

42-43: B

46-47

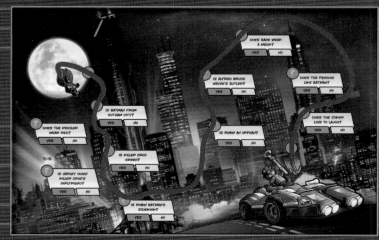

48-49

54-57

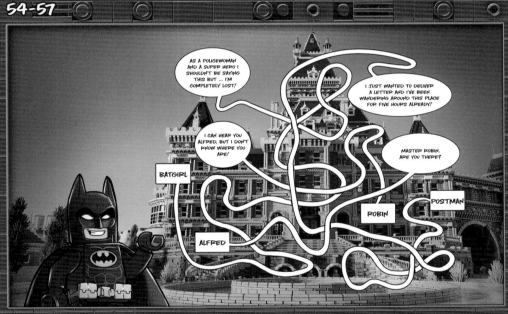

56-57